A Haunted Capital

by Natalie Lunis

Consultant: Troy Taylor
President of the American Ghost Society

BEARPORT
PUBLISHING

New York, New York

Credits

Cover and Title Page, © Viktor Kurya/Fotolia, © olly/Fotolia, © Marcus/Fotolia, © rasstock/Fotolia, © Gary Blakeley/Fotolia; 4–5, © spirit of america/Shutterstock, © Kladej/Shutterstock, © jakgree/Fotolia; 6, © Visions of America, LLC/Alamy; 7T, © Getty Images; 7B, © Sipa Press; 8, © Bettmann/CORBIS; 9T, © The White House Historical Association; 9M, © The Granger Collection, NYC; 9B, © Corbis; 10, © digidreamgrafix/Shutterstock; 11, © The Granger Collection, NYC; 12, © Efrain Padro/Alamy; 13, © epa european pressphoto agency b.v./Alamy; 14, © Bettmann/CORBIS; 15T, © Pictorial Press Ltd/Alamy; 15B, © Shvaygert Ekaterina/Shutterstock; 16, © Orhan Cam/Shutterstock; 17T, © Corbis; 17B, © Elena Schweitzer/Shutterstock; 18, © Philip Scalia/Alamy; 19T, © Courtesy of the Library of Congress; 19B, © Robert C. Lautman/The Octagon; 20L, © Collection of John Deferrari; 20R, © Getty Images; 21, © Cameron Whitman/Thinkstock; 22R, © Richard T. Nowitz/Corbis; 22L, © B Christopher/Alamy; 23T, © Bettmann/CORBIS; 23B, © Geoffrey Clements/Corbis; 24, © Courtesy of the Library of Congress; 25T, © Pictorial Press Ltd/Alamy; 25B, © A.F. Bradley/steamboattimes.com/Wikipedia; 26, © Collection of John Deferrari; 27T, © Virginia Historical Society, Richmond, Virginia/Bridgeman Art Library; 27B, © The Art Gallery Collection/Alamy; 31, © Shutterstock; 32, © Pakhnyushcha/Shutterstock.

Publisher: Kenn Goin
Editorial Director: Adam Siegel
Creative Director: Spencer Brinker
Design: Dawn Beard Creative
Cover: Kim Jones
Photo Researcher: We Research Pictures, LLC

Library of Congress Cataloging-in-Publication Data

Lunis, Natalie.
 A haunted capital / by Natalie Lunis ; consultant, Troy Taylor, president of the American Ghost Society.
      pages cm. — (Scary places: Cities)
 Audience: Age 7 to 12.
 Includes bibliographical references and index.
 ISBN-13: 978-1-62724-243-1 (library binding)
 ISBN-10: 1-62724-243-0 (library binding)
 1. Ghosts—Washington (D.C.)—Juvenile literature. 2. Haunted places—Washington (D.C.)—Juvenile literature. 3. Washington (D.C.)—Social life and customs—Juvenile literature. 4. Washington (D.C.)—Buildings, structures, etc.—Juvenile literature. I. Taylor, Troy. II. Title.
 BF1472.U6L86 2015
 133.109753—dc23
                         2014009034

For more information, write to Bearport Publishing Company, Inc., 45 West 21st Street, Suite 3B, New York, New York 10010. Printed in the United States of America.

10 9 8 7 6 5 4 3 2 1

Contents

Haunted Washington, D.C.

Places that are filled with history are also thought to be filled with ghosts. If that is true, then Washington, D.C.— a city that dates back to the earliest days of the United States of America—is surely one of the most haunted cities in the country.

In this book, you will visit eleven of the most haunted spots in America's **capital** and come across some of its most famous ghosts. Among them are a former president who never left the White House, a vice president who still hurries to his office in the **Capitol** building, and a **First Lady** who has found a quiet and peaceful home—years after her death. Don't be scared when you meet these **spirits**, however. Instead, think of them as guides into America's colorful and exciting past.

Lincoln's Ghosts

The White House, Lincoln Bedroom

The White House is the home of the United States' **elected** leader—the president. For this reason, it is sometimes called "the people's house." Should it also be called "the people's *haunted* house"? After all, many ghosts are said to be found there.

The White House

The most famous ghosts to haunt the White House belong to the Lincoln family. In the winter of 1862, while Abraham Lincoln was serving as president, his eleven-year-old son Willie became ill with **typhoid** and died shortly afterward. Both President Lincoln and his wife, Mary, were filled with **grief**. Mary, who had a strong belief in spirits, soon arranged several **séances** so she could try to contact her son. Less than a year later, she began to see him at night, standing at the foot of her bed.

Abraham Lincoln

In April 1865, about three years after Willie's death, President Lincoln was shot and killed while attending a play at Ford's Theatre in downtown Washington, D.C. Since then, his ghost has been seen inside the White House many times. Most often, it is spotted in a room that was once Lincoln's office.

Years after Lincoln's death, a bed and other pieces of furniture belonging to the Lincolns were brought in to Lincoln's old office. The room became known from that time on as the Lincoln Bedroom. It was a place for very important guests—and, according to some visitors, one very important ghost—to spend the night.

The Lincoln Bedroom

During the 1940s, British Prime Minister Winston Churchill visited the White House and stayed in the Lincoln Bedroom. According to reports, he saw Lincoln's ghost standing near the fireplace. After that, he asked to be moved to another room.

Burned by the British

The White House, Front Doorway

Begun in 1792, the White House was nearly completed in 1800, when the country's second president, John Adams, moved in. Only fourteen years later, however, while President James Madison was living there, the building was nearly burned down. A few signs of the damage remain behind. Some people say a ghost does as well.

This painting shows people running away as the White House and other buildings in Washington, D.C., burned in 1814.

James Madison was the fourth president of the United States. In 1812, during his first term in office, the United States went to war with Great Britain. The war, which was largely over control of the seas, came to be known as the **War of 1812**.

James Madison

In late August of 1814, two years after the start of the war, British soldiers entered Washington, D.C. They set fire to many buildings, including the White House. By the time they left, only the outer walls of the White House remained.

Dolley Madison

The White House was rebuilt and repainted in the years that followed. However, two spots on its outer walls have always been left untouched. The burn marks on them are meant to serve as a reminder of the event that almost destroyed the building about 200 years ago. According to stories, a red-coated British soldier from that time can also be seen. He is usually near the front doorway, carrying either a lantern or a torch. Perhaps the soldier stays behind to make sure that people never forget the dramatic event.

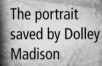

The portrait saved by Dolley Madison

Both James Madison and his wife, First Lady Dolley Madison, had to leave the White House after learning that the British were on the way. Dolley, however, stayed a bit longer than James. She took time to have a life-size portrait of George Washington removed from a wall and safely carried out of the building.

Unfinished Work

United States Capitol, The Senate Building

Located atop a hill near the center of Washington, D.C., the United States Capitol is one of the city's most important buildings. It is where members of both the United States **Senate** and **House of Representatives** meet. These people who make the country's laws may not be the only ones who show up for work there, however. Reportedly, the ghosts of some who first built the Capitol do as well.

The United States Capitol

Work on the United States Capitol began in 1793, while George Washington was president. In later years, parts of the building were redesigned and rebuilt, resulting in the building's current appearance. In its center is a huge **dome**. To the sides of the dome are two main **wings**, or sections. One is known as the Senate wing. The other wing is known as the House of Representatives wing.

According to **legend**, a **stonemason** was killed during the earliest construction of what is now the Senate wing. One version of the story says that he was crushed to death when a wall collapsed and buried him. Another says that he got into an argument with a fellow worker and was killed when the man hit him over the head with a brick. Whether he was the victim of an accident or a murder, some say the stonemason has remained in the basement ever since. Sometimes he is heard banging and scratching from behind a wall. At other times his ghostly figure is seen passing through it.

Pierre Charles L'Enfant was a French engineer hired by George Washington to design plans for the Capitol and other parts of Washington, D.C. Some say he was never paid for his work, however. Since his death, his ghost has reportedly been seen angrily rushing through the hallways of the Capitol, with the plans he drew up under his arm.

This painting shows George Washington (left) and engineer Pierre Charles L'Enfant (center) exploring the area where the Capitol was to be built.

The Dancing Statues

United States Capitol, Statuary Hall

Most of the time, the United States Capitol is a busy place. Hundreds of politicians and members of their staffs work there. Thousands of visitors from all over the country pass through on guided tours. Yet there is one part of the building that is said to come to life only one time each year—after everyone has left and the place seems quiet and empty.

Statuary Hall

Statuary Hall is named for the lifelike statues on display there. However, this grand **semicircular** space was not always meant to be a place for artwork. From 1807 to 1857, it was where the U.S. House of Representatives met. Then, after the members of the House moved to a newer part of the Capitol building, it took on its present name and purpose.

At first, the idea was to have each state send two statues—each representing an important person from the state. Over the years, however, the hall became too crowded. Some of the statues were moved to other parts of the building. Today, there are 38 statues in the hall.

The changes in the pieces of artwork might not be the only comings and goings that have taken place in Statuary Hall. Some people say that every year, at the stroke of midnight on New Year's Eve, the statues step off their pedestals and dance around the beautiful marble-floored room. For a short while, they celebrate another year in the history of the country.

People who work in the Capitol have reported feeling that the statues in the hall seem to follow them with their eyes—especially at night, when the employees are working late.

Killed by a Chill

United States Capitol, Senate Wing

With more than 600 rooms and several miles of hallway, it's not surprising that the Capitol building is home to many ghosts. One of them continues to haunt the part of the building where he worked—and died.

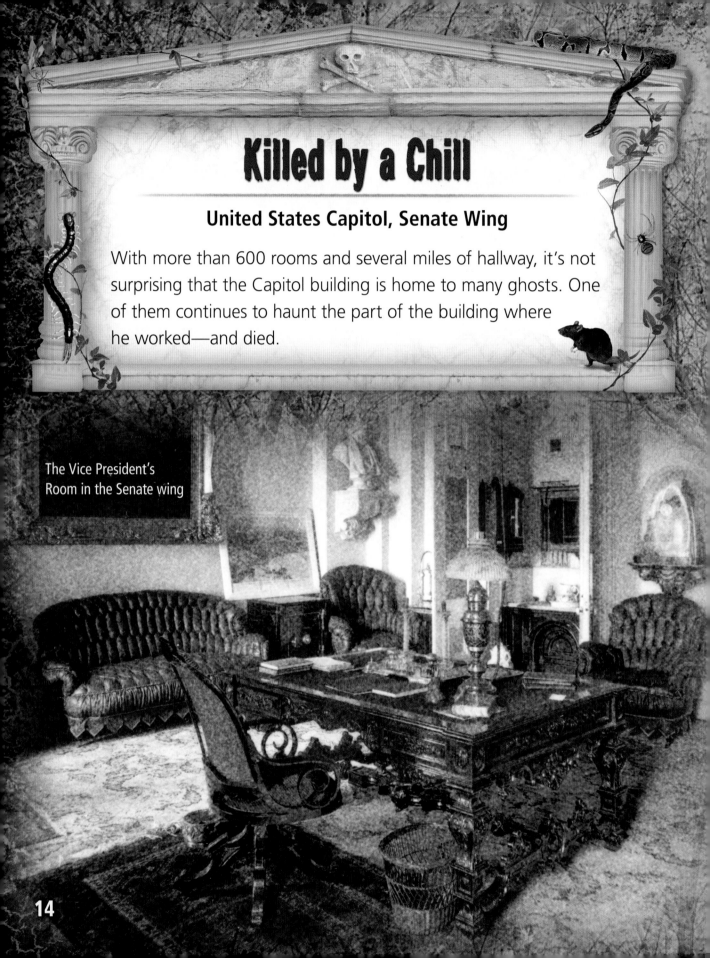

The Vice President's Room in the Senate wing

One of the offices in the United States Capitol belongs to the vice president of the United States. That's because, among other duties, the vice president serves as the head of the United States Senate.

Vice President Henry Wilson

In 1875, Henry Wilson was vice president. He spent much of his time in the vice president's office, but he also spent time in the basement of the Senate, where senators could take baths in bathing rooms at the beginning or end of their long workdays. One very chilly November night, it is said, Wilson fell asleep while in the tub. When he awoke, he wrapped himself in a towel and hurried to his office. Soon after, he became ill and died in his office.

Since Wilson's death, people who work in the Senate have sensed the presence of his ghost in and near his former office. They have heard coughing and sneezing and have even smelled soap. In addition, down in the basement, witnesses have seen a ghostly figure that is wrapped in a towel and hurrying to get upstairs.

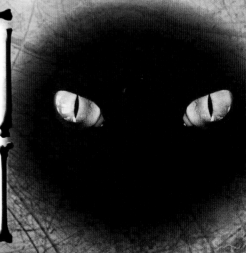

An even scarier sight in the Capitol's basement is the Demon Cat. This spooky creature has been talked about since the 1800s, when real cats patrolled the building in search of rats. Reportedly, the Demon Cat grows to the size of a tiger if anyone comes near it. In addition, it is usually seen just before a **national disaster** or **tragedy**—such as the **assassination** of Abraham Lincoln.

The Library Ghost

Library of Congress

Located just east of the United States Capitol is the Library of **Congress**, where one of the world's largest collections of printed books—as well as letters, pictures, and maps—can be found. A worried ghost is said to walk among these important items. What is he searching for—and why?

Library of Congress

The Library of Congress was started in 1800. Its main purpose was to provide information to members of the United States government. At first, the library's collection was kept in a room in the Capitol building. Later, as the collection grew bigger and bigger, three separate buildings, one next to the other, were constructed to hold it.

The old Library of Congress

According to legend, a worker from the early days of the library did not trust banks. As a result, he hid thousands of dollars between the pages of some of the books. Unfortunately, he died before he could get the money back and spend it. Since his death, he has returned as a ghost to look for it. Some versions of the story say that he's been spotted in the library's old location in the Capitol building. Other versions say that he haunts the new library, forever opening and flipping through books in search of the hidden money.

Sightings of a ghost wearing a police officer's uniform have been reported in the new Library of Congress. The spirit is a helpful one as he is said to guide people when they become lost in the miles of books stacked on shelves.

Washington's Most Haunted

The Octagon House

The word *octagon* means "eight sides." Yet the 200-year-old Octagon House, located in the same Washington neighborhood as the White House, actually has just six sides. That's not the only strange thing about it, however. It is also known as the most haunted house in the city.

Octagon House

The Octagon House was built in 1801. Its first owner, Colonel John Tayloe III, was a wealthy Virginia landowner who was friendly with many American leaders, including George Washington. One day, however, Tayloe learned that his daughter had fallen in love with and planned to marry a young British officer. Like most Americans of his time, Tayloe considered the British to be enemies and so he was completely against the marriage. During an argument about it, his daughter became terribly upset and fell from the top of the house's beautiful spiral staircase. She died as a result.

John Tayloe III

Shockingly, a similar event occurred a few years later. Another of Tayloe's daughters had married a man whom the colonel did not like. When she returned home to try to make peace with the family, she too fell to her death from the top of the stairs.

Following the two tragedies, strange sights and sounds have been reported. Some people have seen the light of a candle traveling up the stairs, as if being carried by an unseen person. Others have heard a scream or a thud and seen a crumpled body on the floor just below the last step.

Many other ghost stories are told about the Octagon House. In some, the spirits of slaves who once lived there show their presence by ringing bells. In others, ghostly servants sometimes appear at the front door, as if ready to greet guests.

The staircase inside the Octagon House

A Star-Spangled Ghost

The Francis Scott Key House and Bridge

As the writer of the **lyrics** of "The Star-Spangled Banner," Francis Scott Key lives on through his famous song. Some people say he also lives on as a ghost in his old Washington neighborhood.

The Francis Scott Key House

Francis Scott Key

During the War of 1812, which was fought between the Americans and the British in and around Washington, D.C., Francis Scott Key was a lawyer living and working in the capital city. He also enjoyed writing poetry. One day, near the end of the war, Key witnessed a British attack on Fort McHenry in Baltimore, Maryland. The event—which ended with the American flag still flying—moved him to write the words for "The Star-Spangled Banner." Many years later, in 1931, the song became the **national anthem** of the United States.

Key's home, which was built for him around 1802, was next to the Potomac River in a neighborhood known as Georgetown. In the late 1800s, long after his death, Key is believed to have returned there. Some say it was because the owners were changing the house to make it more modern and up-to-date. Reportedly, loud footsteps, moans, sighs, and even bloodstains on the attic ceiling were signs of the haunting. The spooky events ended only after new owners **restored** the house to its original style. Had Key's ghost found peace once his home looked as it did when he left it?

The Francis Scott Key Bridge

In 1947, the Francis Scott Key House was torn down in order to make room for a new bridge—which was named for the famous songwriter. Today, people in Washington say that Key's ghost is unhappy about the change and has once more returned to the spot.

The Haunted Pew

St. John's Episcopal Church

From the top of a famous church, a bell **tolls** six times. The ringing tells the people who live in Washington, D.C., that an important person has died. Does it also bring six mysterious ghosts out to **mourn**?

St. John's
Episcopal Church

James Madison, the fourth president of the United States, was leading the country when St. John's **Episcopal** Church was built just across from the White House. He began attending services there and selected a **pew** to sit in during his visits. Since Madison's time, every American president has at one point or another attended the church, sitting in the same spot. As a result, this pew has become known as the "President's pew."

The President's pew

Madison and those elected after him are not the only ones to use this special seating, however. According to legend, every time the church's bell rings to mark the death of a U.S. president or another very important American, six ghostly figures in white robes appear in the pew at midnight. Then, shortly after, they disappear. No one knows who they are, but in some versions of the legend, the figures are said to come out of the six columns that stand at the front of the church. They then go back into them until the sad day when they need to come out again.

The church's bell was made by the Revere Company of Boston. This company was headed by Joseph Revere, who was the son of Paul Revere—a famous hero of the **Revolutionary War**.

A painting of Paul Revere

23

Ghost After Ghost

Halcyon House

During its more than 200-year-long history, Halcyon House has had a number of different owners. The two most famous ones lived very different lives. Today, however, they have something in common—both have returned to the beautiful home as ghosts!

Halcyon House

Benjamin Stoddert was an important **military** leader. From 1798 to 1801, he served as the first **secretary** of the United States Navy. Although his time in office was short, Stoddert added many powerful ships and got the Navy off to a strong start. After leaving the job, however, he suffered poor health. He lived quietly in Halcyon House, an attractive home in the neighborhood of Georgetown, and died there in 1813.

Benjamin Stoddert

Nearly a hundred years later, in 1900, Albert Adsit Clemons bought the house. Clemons had many strange habits and ideas. Most oddly, he believed that as long as he continued to add on to Halcyon House, he would live forever. As a result, he filled the house with many useless doors, stairways, and rooms. Yet these additions did him no good. He died in 1938.

Today, the ghosts of Stoddert and Clemons are said to haunt Halcyon House. Both have appeared in several different rooms, and ghostly footsteps can be heard coming from the attic. No one has been able to say, however, whether or not the two ghosts have ever met.

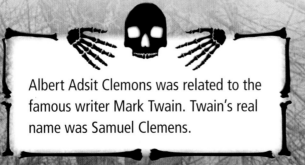

Albert Adsit Clemons was related to the famous writer Mark Twain. Twain's real name was Samuel Clemons.

Mark Twain

Home, Sweet Home

The Cutts-Madison House

It is often said that ghosts are the spirits of people who are unable to find rest after death. That is not true of the ghost that haunts one home in the nation's capital, however. This famous ghost appears quite comfortable whenever she is seen.

The Cutts-Madison House

Dolley Madison lived a life that was filled with action and drama. In 1809, she moved into the White House with her husband, President James Madison. In 1814, when British troops set fire to the building during the War of 1812, the Madisons had to flee and find another home.

Dolley Madison

James Madison died in 1836, and Dolley became a widow. Even though she had once been the First Lady, she struggled to live a comfortable life and pay her bills. In 1837, she moved into the Cutts house, which the Madisons had bought from Richard Cutts, Dolley's brother-in-law. A few years later, Dolley moved to and managed a Virginia farm that she owned. Then in 1843 she moved back to the Cutts House, where she lived until her death in 1849.

Today, the three-story home is known as the Cutts-Madison House. It is also known as the home of Dolley Madison's ghost. At the side of the house, where there used to be a porch, Dolley's ghost has been seen gently rocking in a chair. According to reports, she always greets visitors with a kind and gentle smile.

Dolley Madison's ghost has been a well-known sight for a very long time. During the second half of the 1800s, members of the Washington Club—a club for businessmen and politicians that was located nearby—would tip their hats to the former First Lady whenever they passed by.

Halcyon House

A Navy leader and a man who thought he could live forever share a haunted house.

The Francis Scott Key Bridge

Does the poet who wrote our national anthem haunt this bridge?

The Octagon House

Two young women tumble to their deaths—and return as ghosts.

VIRGINIA

LINCOLN MEMORIAL

POTOMAC RIVER

CANADA

UNITED STATES OF AMERICA

Washington, D.C.

MEXICO

Washington, D.C.

St. John's Episcopal Church

Six ghostly figures turn up during times of tragedy.

The Cutts-Madison House

A former First Lady seems to feel at home here.

The United States Capitol

Watch for a ghostly stonemason, dancing statues, and a demon cat.

The White House

Abraham Lincoln, his son Willie, and a British soldier from the War of 1812 have all been spotted here.

WASHINGTON MONUMENT

The Library of Congress

A ghostly worker searches for hidden money.

JEFFERSON MEMORIAL

Glossary

assassination (uh-*sass*-i-NAY-shuhn) the killing of a famous or politically important person

capital (KAP-uh-tuhl) the city where a state or country's government is based

Capitol (KAP-uh-tuhl) the building in Washington, D.C., where Congress meets

Congress (KON-gruhss) the part of the U.S. government that makes laws; it is made up of the House of Representatives and the Senate

dome (DOHM) the rounded top of a building

elected (i-LEKT-id) chosen by voters

Episcopal (i-PIS-kuh-puhl) a Christian religion

First Lady (FURST LAY-dee) the wife of the U.S. President

grief (GREEF) great sadness

House of Representatives (HOUSS UHV *rep*-ri-ZEN-tuh-tivz) one of the two main groups that make laws for the United States

legend (LEJ-uhnd) a story that is handed down from the past that may be based on fact but is not always completely true

lyrics (LIHR-iks) the words to a song

military (MIL-uh-tair-ee) having to do with the armed forces

mourn (MORN) to feel or express sadness over someone's death

national anthem (NASH-uh-nuhl AN-them) the official song of a country

national disaster (NASH-uh-nuhl duh-ZASS-tur) a sudden event causing much damage, loss, or suffering to an entire country

pew (PYOO) a bench-like seat in a church

restored (ri-STORD) brought back to the original condition

Revolutionary War (*rev*-uh-LOO-shuhn-er-ee WAR) a war fought from 1775 to 1783 in which the American colonies won independence from Great Britain

séances (SAY-ahnss-iz) gatherings for the purpose of communicating with ghosts

secretary (SEK-ruh-*tair*-ee) in government, the head of a department

semicircular (*sem*-ee-SIR-*kyoo*-lur) shaped like half a circle

Senate (SEN-it) one of the two main groups that make laws for the United States

spirits (SPIHR-its) supernatural creatures, such as ghosts

stonemason (STOHN-*mayss*-uhn) someone who works with bricks and stone

tolls (TOHLZ) rings

tragedy (TRAJ-uh-dee) a sad and terrible event

typhoid (TYE-foid) a disease that causes fever, weakness, and headaches

War of 1812 (WAR UHV AY-teen TWELV) a war fought from 1812 to 1815 between the United States and Great Britain, largely over control of the seas and shipping routes

wings (WINGZ) sections that are attached to the main part of a building

Bibliography

Hauck, Dennis William. *Haunted Places: The National Directory.* New York: Penguin Books (2002).

Kiger, Patrick, J. "The Story of Lincoln's Ghost." (http://channel .nationalgeographic.com/channel/killing-lincoln/articles/the-story-of-lincolns -ghost/)

Krepp, Tim. *Capitol Hill Haunts (Haunted America).* Charleston, SC: The History Press (2012).

Wetzel, Charles. *Haunted U.S.A.* New York: Sterling (2008).

Read More

Bellanger, Jeff. *Who's Haunting the White House? The President's Mansion and the Ghosts Who Live There.* New York: Sterling (2008).

Cohen, Daniel. *Ghost in the House.* New York: Scholastic (1995).

Williams, Dinah. *Haunted Houses (Scary Places).* New York: Bearport (2008).

Learn More Online

To learn more about haunted Washington, D.C., visit
www.bearportpublishing.com/ScaryPlaces

Index

About the Author

Natalie Lunis has written many nonfiction books for children. She lives in New York's lower Hudson River Valley—the home of the Headless Horseman.